Born in 1950, **Rowan Williams** was educated in Swansea (Wales) and Cambridge. He studied for his theology doctorate in Oxford, after which he taught theology in a seminary near Leeds. From 1977 until 1986 he was engaged in academic and parish work in Cambridge, before returning to Oxford as Lady Margaret Professor of Divinity. In 1990 he became a Fellow of the British Academy.

In 1992 Professor Williams became Bishop of Monmouth, and in 1999 he was elected as Archbishop of Wales. He became Archbishop of Canterbury in late 2002 with ten years' experience as a diocesan bishop and three as a primate in the Anglican Communion. As Archbishop, his main responsibilities were pastoral – whether leading his own diocese of Canterbury and the Church of England or guiding the Anglican Communion worldwide.

At the end of 2012, after ten years as Archbishop, he stepped down and moved to a new role as Master of Magdalene College, Cambridge, from which he retired in September 2020. Professor Williams is acknowledged internationally as an outstanding theological writer and teacher as well as an accomplished poet and translator. His interests include music, fiction and languages.

D1340243

CANDLES IN THE DARK

Faith, hope and love
in a time of pandemic

Rowan Williams

First published in Great Britain in 2020

Society for Promoting Christian Knowledge
36 Causton Street
London SW1P 4ST
www.spck.org.uk

British Library Cataloguing-in-Publication Data
A catalogue record for this book is available from the British Library

ISBN 978-0-281-08596-5
eBook ISBN 978-0-281-08597-2

1 3 5 7 9 10 8 6 4 2

Typeset by The Book Guild Ltd, Leicester
First printed in Great Britain by
CPI Group (UK) Ltd, Croydon, CR0 4YY

eBook by The Book Guild Ltd, Leicester

Produced on paper from sustainable forests

Contents

Preface   ix

A change has begun   1
A clearer vision   4
Staying put   7
All times belong to him   10
Fragile trust   13
We are not alone   16
Life beyond lockdown   19
A steady solidarity   23
At the still centre   27
We are not God   30
Keep yourselves from idols   33
Online communion   36
The problem with statues   40
Second nature   44
Meditative walking   47
Power to be free   50
Behind the mask   54
At home in the world   58
Liturgy in life   62
Transfiguration   66
To be born again   70
The rule of the algorithm   74
Praying for Jerusalem   78
Law and order   82
The presence of the past   86
Herd mentality   90

Epilogue   94

Preface

Local churches have responded in a variety of creative ways to the challenges of the COVID-19 pandemic; and for many congregations this has opened an unexpected door into new kinds of collaboration and involvement. The small church of St Clement's near the city centre in Cambridge has been mounting a live-streamed Eucharist every Sunday from the home of one of the associated clergy, with a time for online discussion afterwards. It has also created a daily bulletin for prayers and news, with suggested biblical readings, an assortment of people's photographic meditations, and a short reflection. These reflections have been written by members of the congregation as well as clergy who minister at the church, and others who have a more occasional connection with its life. They have been an important factor in keeping the community together. The service and the bulletin have drawn a sizeable and varied group of people keen to explore the resources of faith in a time of crisis.

Before my recent move back to Wales I had the privilege of assisting regularly at St Clement's, and was grateful for the opportunity to contribute weekly to this venture. The meditations in this little book represent six months of these weekly offerings. What these pages don't show is the steady underlying stream of shared reflection on the part of a significant number of others, lay and ordained, who have supported the initiative by writing for the bulletin more or less regularly. I want to pay tribute to the insight and commitment of all of them, and to acknowledge how much what is set down here owes to the ongoing conversation with the St Clement's community. I also want to thank Sarah and Robert van de Weyer for all their work in organising the daily bulletin and weekly worship for St Clement's over these months, and for the encouragement they and others have given in bringing these meditations together.

The church has a long Catholic Anglican tradition, and still uses the language of the Book of Common Prayer, which will explain why the quotations here from biblical and liturgical texts are often in traditional language; and what I've written generally takes for granted a certain kind of practice and vocabulary. I hope this doesn't get in the way for readers who are not native to this environment. I'm always encouraged by the fact that the worship at St Clement's seems to speak to people from a wide variety of social and national backgrounds and a representative spread of ages; so I have not tried to remove what is specific to this congregation any more than I have edited out local references to the city and its landscape, hoping that a wider readership 'overhearing' this will still find things they recognise and resonate with.

We are by no means out of the wood yet as far as the pandemic is concerned. What we have been thinking and praying about in these last months as reflected here is, sadly, not a matter of historical interest. The acute challenges to faith, hope and love remain. But these meditations – brief and scrappy as they may be – are offered in the hope that our Christian communities will continue to find resources of compassion, trust and energy to share with a society and a world struggling with what seem unmanageable burdens and impossibly complex decisions.

Rowan Williams
26 October, 2020

26 March

A change has begun

'As we contemplate the coming months, not knowing when we can breathe again, it's worth thinking about how already the foundations have been laid for whatever new opportunities God has for us on the far side of this crisis.'

Yesterday we remembered the Annunciation – the real beginning of the human life of Jesus, that microscopic change in the physiology of a young woman in Nazareth that is the hinge on which the history of the world turns.

What did Mary think and feel on the day after the message of her unique destiny? I very much doubt whether she felt that the world had been transfigured around her. She would not even yet feel the new life growing within her; and she would have good reason to be anxious about her pregnancy – about the reaction of her fiancé in the short term, and in the longer term about the huge and obscure burden she had been asked to carry in nurturing into life the divine Redeemer.

No signs of change; but a change has begun. The story has started to unfold, and without that almost invisible beginning in the depths of Mary's body there would be no story – no Christmas, no Good Friday, no Easter. We can go back even further and think how all the history that leads up to Mary herself is also part of the same reality: the long history of the Jewish people in all its detail, the mysterious and completely hidden process by which Mary grew into a human openness and generosity that was free enough to welcome the promise of God into her own physical reality. All this is what makes Jesus possible.

And here we are, in the middle of the most penitential Lent you could imagine, looking around for signs of a transfigured world; looking around what seems a wasteland, with no timetable to reassure us that things will be back to normal any time soon. We can't do what we'd normally do to show our devotion; we can't gather in celebration and share the food and drink of God's Kingdom in the atmosphere of joy and beauty that we take for granted in worship. We can't even sing together.

But the story that began in Mary's body, that began even further back in God's call to Adam and Abraham and Moses, is a story that has begun in us. We have been brought into that new reality, whether or not we feel it stirring, whether or not we see the signs of its presence in the ways we've got used to. The sacramental life of Christ's Body is alive in us; even if all we can do is associate ourselves with the celebration of the Eucharist somewhere else, through some sort of remote electronic contact, the life is there, the connection is there.

And as we contemplate the coming months, not knowing when we can breathe again, it's worth thinking about how already the foundations have been laid for whatever new opportunities God has for us on the far side of this crisis. The small actions we take to protect one another, to keep open the channels of love and gift, volunteering, if we're able, to support someone less mobile or less safe, finding new ways of communicating, even simply meditating on how our society might become more just and secure – all this can be the hidden beginning of something fuller and more honest for us all in the future.

The God who begins the story of his world-shattering life in the midst of creation with that tiny, imperceptible change in the body of Mary, is still a God who works with tiny and hidden changes. In each of us, body and spirit, that same God is working now, so that Christmas and Good Friday and Easter will come alive in us, in ways we can't begin to imagine.

2 April

A clearer vision

'It's only when the vague, drifting muddle of the way we
usually think about ourselves is blown away by the Spirit
that we see the underlying contours – the deep needs, the
ingrained resistances, the aching hopes and loves.'

As I was taking the bin out the other night, I was struck
by the extreme clarity of the night sky – a crisply outlined
moon and stars, Venus glowing steadily to the north-west
– and it reminded me of something I'd recently heard
about how aerial photographs of China had been showing a
dramatic drop in levels of pollution. You could actually see
more of the contours of the landmass and the shape of roads
and cities because the sky was clearer.

Now I doubt whether a fine night in Cambridge has
much to do with any measurable drop in atmospheric
pollution locally (though the BBC website does tell me that
such a drop is happening). But – just as when you have a
chance to look at the night sky perhaps on holiday, from
a beach or a hilltop – it's always sobering to realize just
how much of it we miss, whether by simply not looking
or because we are so accustomed to light pollution in our
urban landscapes.

There are times when it's as if a whole layer of mess

4

and mist and drifting fumes is cleared away and we see things in their proper outlines – around us on the ground as well as in the heavens. Just at the moment, with so few folk out of doors, even an ordinary walk down the street in Cambridge can uncover an angle or an aspect of some view, some building, some turn of the river, that you'd never seen, or at least never registered. A few days ago, I was delighted to see one young runner on Jesus Green suddenly stop and pull out a phone to photograph a spray of blossom.

Layers removed: it's another image for what Lent and Passiontide are about. We try to let some kind of sharp, cleansing wind blow through the fog of idleness and selfishness, so that the landscape of our spirits stands out more clearly. Not that it's always a pretty sight; not many sprays of blossom to stop someone in their tracks. But it's only when the vague, drifting muddle of the way we usually think about ourselves is blown away by the Spirit that we see the underlying contours – the deep needs, the ingrained resistances, the aching hopes and loves.

So yes, this is a season for seeing ourselves more clearly – the season of Passiontide, but also the season of separation and being driven in on ourselves that we're living through collectively. Yet the truth about Passiontide is deeper still. We can see the sky. A curtain has been torn down, not just the veil over our own faces (as St Paul so wonderfully puts in 2 Corinthians 3), but the veil that covers the face of God in our imaginations – the drift of fantasies and projections about God that can keep us both comfortable and frightened all at once. The sky is clear and what is visible in the cross and resurrection of Jesus is the steady radiance of an endless love that is focused on our healing and well-being; as sharply defined as moon and stars and beautiful Venus against the dark.

9 April

Maundy Thursday

Staying put

'To obey the new commandment of love is to stay put: to
stay with the people God has given us to love, to nurture and
be nurtured by, to challenge and be challenged by.'

The poet W. H. Auden once wrote that it was easy enough
to say 'I will love you forever'; the difficult thing was to say
(and mean), 'I will love you at 4.15 next Thursday.' How do
we go on loving, making the love real in every moment,
when moods and circumstances change our feelings or sap
our energy?

Maundy Thursday commemorates the command, the
mandatum, given by Jesus: love one another as I have loved
you. And perhaps the clue is in those words, *as I have loved
you*. Jesus, says the Gospel narrative, loves 'to the end'; he
does not falter or turn away. We know this love, not because
Jesus is always telling us how much he feels for us, but in
the simple fact that he stays there, for us and with us. Even
when his friends run away, he does not forget or abandon
them. Think of his words from the cross to the disciple he
loves, as he 'adopts' him into his family by declaring Mary
to be the disciple's mother too. The resurrection is in one

way a story about how Jesus never leaves those he loves, and never changes the way he relates to them.

So to obey the new commandment of love is to stay put: to stay with the people God has given us to love, to nurture and be nurtured by, to challenge and be challenged by. The summons to stay put has an extra layer of significance this year, and we may well give a wry smile at it. But the truth is that we betray love ultimately not by feelings of impatience or even hostility, but by the desire to be somewhere else with people and circumstances other than the ones actually in front of our noses – by saying to God, in effect, Can we have a nicer and more manageable world, please, with people that it's easier to love?

Of course this doesn't mean we don't seek to change our world for the better; it certainly doesn't mean that we put up with or collude with situations of injustice, violence or abuse. But we always have to begin by engaging with what's actually there, not dreaming of a world where it's all so much simpler.

Jesus shows that he is 'with us always even to the end of the age' (as he says at the end of St Matthew's Gospel) by rising from the dead and giving us the gift of his life in the Holy Spirit. And the regular sign of this in the Church's life is the Holy Eucharist: we gather and pray in the Spirit and the life of Jesus is *there*, in us and in the bread and wine that stand for the gifts of all creation, reconciled and renewed through Christ, given to us so that we feed and grow. Maundy Thursday is the day when we recall the institution of the Eucharist, and we can rightly see this as above all the sign of a God who does not go away, who keeps his promise to be there with and for us – and so as the sacrament not only of Jesus' passion but of his resurrection.

In an 'ordinary' Holy Week, we'd be keeping watch tonight at the Altar of Repose – 'staying put' with Jesus in his agony as he 'stays put' with us in his dying and rising and his eternal prayer to the Father. The reserved sacrament speaks powerfully of the steady and unfailing presence of Christ in the heart of his Church.

He will not go away. He draws our thanksgiving and adoration in the sacrament. And this year we are called very specially to acknowledge and adore his presence even when the usual physical access to the sacrament is not possible. Here too he is with us – in our homes and our hearts. He is where the Body of Christ is.

And his faithful staying there summons *us* to a life of faithful love and accompaniment – being there for our neighbours, in whatever unexpected way becomes possible in these anything but ordinary times. 'Love one another', says the Lord,' as I have loved you': pray that the Spirit gives strength for us to be Eucharistic signs of the love that stays – so that the whole world may know itself to be accompanied, held and treasured.

16 April

All times belong to him

'In every moment, every encounter, in times of boredom, anger and anxiety, Jesus is with us, offering himself to us.'

It's easy to feel in the present situation that we are *wasting time*. Those of us used to a full and even stressful schedule find it hard to adjust to new rhythms – which sometimes means a rather baffling alternation between great busyness online and then hours of Nothing Very Much. Rather more seriously, those whose working future looks dangerously uncertain have to live with the sense that there is nothing they can do to secure that future, and that what lies immediately ahead is a period in which they can do nothing to protect themselves from the looming threat of unemployment when restrictions begin to be lifted.

The pain of this kind of insecurity is real, and no one can magic it away – though we may be grateful that both government and employers are waking up to the need for more robust safety nets than ever. But meanwhile, how can we stay 'anchored' day by day? How can we face and try to deal with the fear and frustration of time slipping through our hands?

One of the things that Easter declares is that our world of time and change has been transformed by the event of Jesus' resurrection. When we say that Jesus is risen, we mean that there is no sense in which he belongs to the past; his life is never over. When we celebrate the Eucharist, we don't put flowers on a memorial slab; we meet a living and active presence. And if his life is not over in time, neither is it confined in space. The Easter stories in the New Testament suggest that, again and again, the disciples are startled to meet Jesus; he turns up in unexpected places.

In other words, if what we say of him is true, then – as we say in the prayer for the blessing of the Paschal Candle at the Easter Vigil – 'All times belong to him'. In every moment, every encounter, in times of boredom, anger and anxiety, Jesus is with us, offering himself to us. He is present, saying, 'This moment matters: it is a moment in which you can grow a bit – or shrink a bit – as a human being. It is a moment in which my love is there for you, and my invitation to life is set before you. Don' t panic because you're not in control. Your precious humanity is in my hands, and I am ready to give you what is needed to assure you of your dignity and beauty and worth.'

The challenge of faith is – among lots of other things, of course – the challenge to believe this not just at times when life feels 'meaningful', but at times when the climate is overshadowed, the temperature is low and the future obscure. 'All times belong to him': there is nowhere and no-when that is simply 'waste' because the living Jesus is present and active wherever we turn.

This doesn't cancel the pain and anxiety: it simply tells us that each moment is grounded in the divine act that creates and heals. Even if all we can do is – through gritted teeth – acknowledge that God in Christ has promised to be with us to the end of time, we shall have turned just a little away from the idea that for time to be meaningful it has to be packed solid with productive human activity. Just for a moment, we have recognized that the time we live through is lived through with us by our Creator and Lover; its meaning is in his constant presence and his unceasing giving, inviting, welcoming. Our times are in his hand (Ps.31.17 in the Book of Common Prayer), and all our history is pervaded by the light of Easter.

23 April

Fragile trust

'We trust those who are inspired by a vision of something bigger than themselves but who also recognize the ever-present possibility of failing and messing things up.'

One of the disturbing effects of our current crisis that has not yet been fully recognized is that it plays into a deeply negative and destructive message that was already gaining traction in other ways. This is the widespread cynicism and mistrust towards government that in the last ten years or so has grown so rapidly. If we haven't yet *quite* stopped believing anything any politician says, our expectations of clarity and truthfulness are now at a very low point indeed.

The trouble is that it's hard to trust anyone who seems to be obsessively anxious about themselves. We read about leaders and administrators whose first question in the face of a disaster or a hard decision is 'How will this make me look?' Their eyes are not on the realities of the situation, on the flesh and blood need or suffering they are called to confront, but on themselves. And if they are so desperately insecure as to need constant affirmation, why should I feel secure about their judgement or their vision? The paradoxical thing is that we may be more likely to trust someone who is able to say, 'I made a mistake' – because it takes strength to admit that you took a risk and that you are not infallible.

The Gospels tell us about all sorts of different meetings between the disciples and the risen Jesus; and one of the strangest is the story of Doubting Thomas. He doesn't *trust* his fellow disciples when they speak about the resurrection – as if he suspects that they are making something up to reassure themselves. After all, he knows as well as anyone the fear and confusion they all showed when Jesus was arrested.

Jesus appears to him and tells him not to be mistrustful; you don't have to see everything in order to believe, and those who trust without seeing the full picture are called 'blessed.' – that's to say, they are in tune with the truth, they are rightly related to God. He seems to be saying to Thomas and to us that we must learn to trust one another – and that if the resurrection is going to be credible, the witnesses of the resurrection must be human beings who are *credible*, who are not obsessed with themselves and their security, their status, their certainty. People start believing in the resurrection when they see Christians whose nervousness and self-concern has been overtaken by a sense of joyful promise so intense that it can feel frightening. What converts people is not argument or assertion but the sight of human lives 'surprised by joy'. Perhaps Thomas's problem was that when he looked at the faces of his old friends and companions, only a week after the first Easter morning, he saw them already slipping back into their old anxieties and rivalries, their joy already getting a bit wobbly.

But he needed Jesus to say to him, 'Yes, these friends of

yours and mine aren't totally changed overnight. But don't give way to cynicism. Like you, these are fragile folk who get things wrong and sometimes run away from the truth. But look at them again: they are still here with each other, still committed to each other, still living in hope that they can grow and change further if they go on being faithful and trustful with each other. Now it's time for you to take the risk of committing yourself to this fragile community and doing what you can to keep the joy alive and make the message credible.'

It's a word we could all do with hearing. And it does have a connection with where we started. We trust those who are inspired by a vision of something bigger than themselves *but who also recognize the ever-present possibility of failing and messing things up* – and yet they aren't paralysed by that recognition but are still ready to take risks and pay loving attention to the reality around them. When we have a few more people in public life who can live like that, we shall have started to turn the tide of cynicism. God grant that we learn something of all this in the challenges of these times.

30 April
We are not alone

'Just as each one of us can only become who we are in relation to others, so the human race can only be its true self in relation with the rest of the living world.'

One result of our current crisis that's being reported from time to time is the increased boldness of wild animals returning to or extending their habitats – dolphins in the canals of Venice, matched locally by green woodpeckers in the Master's garden at Magdalene, and companionable blackbirds in the churchyard. Many people are able to hear all kinds of birdsong clearly for the first time in years.

Noticing this isn't just a sentimental 'ahh' moment. A leading Canadian poet, Jan Zwicky, wrote a year or two ago about the *loneliness* of human beings in a world that they are rapidly stripping of countless forms of animal and plant life, and suggested that part of the malaise of the contemporary mind was that we were feeling 'homesick' for the company of other life forms – but that we weren't very keen to admit it.

This seems to make a lot of sense. The biblical story begins in a garden full of diverse forms of life; and the first thing Adam is asked to do is to name the animals – to recognize them as part of a world that he shares. Hebrew scripture celebrates, especially in the Psalms and the various 'Wisdom' books, this diversity. In the book of Job, God points to the sheer abundance and variety of animal life, from ostriches to hippos and sea monsters, to remind Job and us that we may have a distinctive place in creation but that we can't expect to domesticate it, any more than we can domesticate its Maker by having tidy and simple ideas about Him.

The first violin in an orchestra is a key person; but they'd look and sound very odd if they were playing alone, or if they were playing something completely independent of the music everyone else was engaged with. Our culture is increasingly looking and sounding like that. We think of and often experience the world as no more than a backdrop to our desires and concerns; and we end up playing a different piece of music. At the present rate, we shall have lost a large section of the orchestra very soon; the prospect is very real of the human race playing a solo as the Titanic goes down, wrecked by our indifference and greed.

It's not at all surprising that many kinds of trauma and dysfunction are addressed these days by involving people in the care of animals. I have a long-standing link with a charity in South Wales which takes young people who have been in Young Offender institutions and hosts them on a farm, where they learn about taking care of horses and cows and pigs. The effects are extraordinary: these rootless youngsters, many of whom have found it very hard to make relationships with other human beings, blossom and flourish as carers for animals - and learn more about human relations too.

We are meant to meet God and to serve God within a rich diversity of organic life; we are human when we are not just confined to human company, human-made environments, artificial stimulants and sedatives. We belong with this animate and animated world, a world we may 'name' and seek to understand but never control. If our culture puts us at a greater and greater distance from this world, we become less human. Just as each one of us can only become who we are in relation to others, so the human race can only be its true self in relation with the rest of the living world.

No wonder we are 'homesick'. We are not just missing a pleasant bit of stage scenery; we are missing ourselves, our real place in creation alongside so many other life-forms. Jesus appears first to Mary Magdalene in a garden, and she thinks he is the gardener. So he is, of course; and he is the new Adam, setting us free from our stupid mythologies of our human uniqueness and omnipotence to embrace a real world once again, a world with room in it for lives that are not ours – human and non-human.

And making room for those other lives is ultimately part of how we make room for the strangest and most wonderful 'otherness' of all – the life of God in its bewildering and sometimes even terrifying abundance. Are we going to remember this when the crisis is past? 'Note to self', as they say...

7 May

Life beyond lockdown

'Will the end of the lockdown see us finding the strength to face and name some of the things that have stood in the way of fairness, truth and security?'

Tomorrow is the 75th anniversary of the end of the Second World War in Europe; and inevitably the language of war and victory will have new echoes for us in our current struggles and troubles. Those who first celebrated VE Day were emerging from what is for most of us now an unimaginable trial: six years of privation and uncertainty and mortal danger. They longed for rest, normality, a return to what they could cope with. And for many people, that's what victory means: the threat is over, all is well once more.

But what's most remarkable about the post-war period is that so many were not satisfied with this alone. For them, victory was *opportunity*: something new had become thinkable. The terrible conflict they had so steadfastly endured had not just been about protection but about clearing the way for change. And within just a few years, the social map of Britain had indeed changed drastically. This country had become a safer place for the sick, the poor and the elderly.

We shouldn't idealize the Welfare State or the personalities who created it, of course; it wasn't a straightforward step into the Kingdom of Heaven, and its creation was – like all political adventures – bound up with compromises, confusions and false starts. Yet it remains true that after six draining years of warfare, people somehow found the energy to face and to name some of the great obstacles to fairness and security that still disfigured British society. The victory that had been won became a source of creativity.

And that's a central aspect of what we say at Easter. 'The strife is o'er, the battle done' we sing on Easter Day, and in the most important sense of all, yes, it is. The death and resurrection of Jesus have made all the difference to the human world, opening the floodgates of divine mercy. But on Easter Day we also remember how Jesus breathes on the apostles and bestows the Holy Spirit: the apostolic community is given the divine energy that will allow them to go and make a difference, announcing forgiveness and renewal, witnessing to God's purpose for humanity in the loving mutuality of the Body of Christ, unveiling in every human face the hidden reflection of God's glory. The *point* of the victory is new creation, the Spirit once again hovering over chaos to bring an ordered world to light.

So we may well think back to 1945 and ask what kind of victory we pray and long for on the far side of the pandemic. As the very first cautious signs of relaxing the lockdown are being talked about, what is it that we long for? A situation where the threat is over and it's back to where we were? Or something more like what the victors of 1945 committed themselves to?

Will the end of the lockdown see us finding the strength to face and name some of the things that have stood in the way of fairness, truth and security? That would mean noticing who has been paying the heaviest price – the ethnic communities and social groups that have been disproportionately affected; the people with mental health challenges who have had to live through nightmares in isolation; under-protected and poorly rewarded workers in the NHS and elsewhere who have had little choice but to go on exposing themselves to risk so that the rest of us can have some basic amenities; young people whose employment prospects have disappeared overnight. If these have paid most heavily, we have to ask what needs doing to guarantee a better deal for them.

And – as government advisers have been saying this week with surprising clarity – will the post-lockdown world be able to think again about all the habits of energy consumption that have had to change during this period? Will we be set free to think afresh about a greener future? Because time is running out, and we have been reminded that a future of environmental crisis is one in which the risks of all sorts of pandemic disease will only become worse.

Above all, though, we who share the Easter faith will be reminded that the resurrection of the Lord is a beginning, not an end – an event that changes for ever the landscape in which we live. The resurrection sets free the Holy Spirit who empowers us to forgive, to speak to and understand the stranger, to build a community of mutual creative service, and to enter into the fullest intimacy with the God who loves us so passionately and unceasingly. If we let ourselves be renewed in the Spirit in all these ways, we shall be ready to take our part in whatever creative newness lies ahead for our society – and by God's grace we shall have won a bit of a victory over our persistent longing to get back into our comfort zone.

14 May

A steady solidarity

'There is heroism in the daily rhythm; making the small differences you can make, at home, online, wherever, in small courtesies and kindnesses, in assuring others they are not alone.'

Today, as you will no doubt know, is the Feast of St Matthias; a saint who has a good claim to be one of the most obscure figures in the entire calendar. We know nothing but his name and the fact that he had been a regular follower of Jesus – and the fact that he was chosen (by the equivalent of tossing a coin) to fill the vacant spot in the apostolic company vacated by Judas Iscariot.

Really not a very impressive start for an apostle – and quite a strange beginning for a book called *The Acts of the Apostles*. Another kind of writer might have been signalling that this hitherto unknown man was going to become a hero of the faith, the brave new face of the Twelve: no one had heard of him up to then, but afterwards, ah well... Only no one seems to have heard of him afterwards either. And the real hero of Acts is of course the most unlikely person of all, not even on the horizon at this point when the book begins: the angry young militant, Saul of Tarsus, sworn enemy of everything to do with Jesus.

You do wonder whether Luke is doing it deliberately. After all, he begins his Gospel by introducing us to a number of elderly eccentrics (Zechariah, Simeon, Anna) who promptly vanish from the story. Yet the story needs them: they set the scene, they pitch the note for the choir to sing. Is Matthias there for the same sort of purpose? Should we sense his obscure presence throughout, in the margins of the great chronicle of Paul's conversion and mission?

Perhaps Luke is saying, 'Don't get over-excited about the heroism of Paul; the fullness of the apostolic witness includes those whose only contribution is that they have lived faithfully in the company of Jesus. There are those who betray and run away, and there are those who just stay. For every tragic Judas and for every blazingly charismatic Paul there is at least one Matthias, quietly hanging in there.' The note that gives the pitch for this story is that steady quietness – curiously mirrored in the subdued ending of Acts, Paul under house arrest, arguing in a desultory way with local rabbis, sharing the faith forcefully with anyone who turns up, but with no public drama.

One of the benefits of having a calendar of saints is that these wildly different lives speak to us in different situations and at different moments. Sometimes we need to be jolted out of toxic smugness and inspired to take some risks; sometimes we need to be shown how someone can live through terrible suffering without either passivity or complaint; and sometimes we need to be reminded that 90 per cent of life is just turning up, as the saying goes. And that too can be apostolic and holy.

We can be very dismissive sometimes of those who

'just turn up'. Enthusiastic missioners naturally want our churches to be packed with ultra-committed folk ready to take to the streets. Doctrinal purists wince when regular churchgoers say they're not too sure what they believe, or when newcomers arrive and hang around at the back reluctant to take the plunge. Yet I'm often struck by the bare fact of how so many turn up in *trust* – trust that they will be welcome, trust that there is something worthwhile in all this, trust that the community will 'carry' them as and when they need – and trust also to commend this to others and welcome them in their turn.

It's not the whole picture; but it's not nothing. Is Matthias the patron saint of the doggedly unspectacular turners-up and hangers-on? Sometimes when we (clergy especially) talk about mission and the need for growth, we give the message that those who actually bother to be there in the first place aren't quite interesting enough and we'd like different people (younger, livelier, cleverer...). Nothing wrong with growth, for goodness' sake; but we should also recognize a faith and even a holiness in those who simply stay in company, share the burdens unobtrusively and do their apostolic bit just by that steady solidarity.

The present crisis is an agonising trial for all those who think that there ought to be a quick fix for everything. At present there isn't a clear way out, there isn't a definitive solution, there isn't even a timetable. Flannel and muddle seem to pour out of most of our political leaders. Young people especially are faced with a far worse challenge than most of us older ones, a real wilderness in which all expectations of work and security are evaporating. There is heroism in the daily rhythm; making the small differences you can make, at home, online, wherever, in small courtesies and kindnesses, in assuring others they are not alone. Maybe that's all Matthias ever did – an undramatic routine of kindness, attentiveness and willingness to put one foot in front of the other. You could say that the one thing that made him memorable among the apostles was that he was The One Who Wasn't Judas. But there are worse epitaphs than being remembered as one who didn't betray and flee. It's a grace we might all reasonably pray for; and when we see steady quiet solidarity in our neighbours, it's a gift we might all well give thanks for.

21 May

Ascension Day

At the still centre

'The traditional icon of the Ascension shows us
simply what always lives in the centre: the stillness
out of which Christ comes to life in the Spirit.'

From as early as the sixth century, the standard way of representing the Lord's Ascension in the Christian East has been to show in the foreground the living and present Body of Christ – Christ's apostles – while the enthroned figure of Christ in glory is depicted on a smaller scale as if receding into heaven. Front and centre is Our Lady, her hands raised in the timeless gesture of prayer – a still, monumental figure among the apostles, who are shown waving their arms and looking thoroughly disoriented.

Now we have no evidence in the Bible that Mary was present at the Ascension (if anything, St Luke's wording rather suggests she wasn't). But that is not the point: her stillness and empty-handedness represent what is at the heart of the Church. Her open hands do not actually touch the circle of light in which the ascended Jesus sits, but they echo and embrace its lines – as if the Church's prayer is shaped by the reality of Jesus glorified, but never grabs it or encompasses it or possesses it.

All the excitement flows around Mary, and yet seems not to touch her. The apostles are bewildered, animated; you can almost hear their heated questioning. Has Jesus really left them for good? What did he mean by saying that he was 'going to his Father'? What did the angels mean when they said he would come again as they had seen him go? Mary in contrast simply extends her hands, as if in readiness to carry the globe of light that is her Son in splendour. Just as in Nazareth, she prepares herself to hold the gift that is Jesus. She opens herself to the Spirit who brings Jesus to birth.

So this is not a 'parting', even if the apostles are inclined to think it is. The same Spirit who brought Jesus to life in Mary's body is doing what the Spirit always does, opening a space in us for the glory of the Word of God to come alive. And this is happening even when the apostles are shaken and confused: somewhere in the middle of the Church – and in the middle of our own lives of faith – there is a pool of still water, ready to receive the image, the light, of Christ afresh.

When we think about the Church we can think about its divisions and controversies. We can – at the moment – think about the rather ill-tempered debates raging online as to whether our Archbishops were right until very recently to prevent clergy from entering their churches. We can find any amount of drama, mess and soap opera. But the traditional icon of the Ascension shows us simply what always lives in the centre: the stillness out of which Christ comes to life in the Spirit. If we pray for the renewal of our faith, it must be a prayer for reconnection with that austere but gentle figure of the Mother of God opening her hands in peace and hopefulness.

We are privileged at times to see in the life of the Church someone who embodies this – it may be a contemplative monk or nun, it may be an unknown layperson, or a child at prayer, or a whole community of worshippers caught up together in quiet loving attention as they hear words or music that open heaven to them. But when this happens, what we see is the real mystery of the Ascension. Christ is no longer present to us as another individual, even a supremely loveable and holy one; he is the life that floods the entire universe. And for us to live, to grow up into our full humanity, we need to be flooded by his life, so that it is 'born' in us as it was in Mary. And we need not to be hypnotized by the soap operas of the Church as an institution. The living Body of Christ on earth is anchored at a far deeper level in that prayer of stillness – the clear and calm water in which the likeness of Christ appears.

28 May

We are not God

'Part of the truth that the Spirit communicates to us is the knowledge that we're not God. If we think we are, we will end up seeking to exterminate the true God, because we see God as our deadly enemy, our dangerous competitor.'

'I have yet many things to say unto you, but ye cannot bear them now', says Jesus in St John's Gospel (16.12). The Spirit of truth whose coming is foretold in these verses will unfold things that cannot yet be said.

So what *is* said when the Spirit comes? According to Acts 2, it's anything but a convenient clarifying postscript to Jesus' teaching; it is the explosion of chaotic noise that occurs as languages and cultures meet and begin to communicate around Jesus. The disciples before the crucifixion and resurrection are not able to bear this level of creative disruption. But what Jesus has to 'say' to the world is the very fact that a worldwide community is possible: the disciples at the Last Supper may not have been be able to digest the idea, but the way Jesus is going to speak in the world from now on is in the community gathered around his cross and resurrection. Not so much in its teaching and example but in the sheer newness of this kind of community, in which we trust one another enough to learn from one another, whatever the gulfs of understanding and culture that divide us.

But it is still the reality of *Jesus* that is communicated, learned, discovered and rediscovered in all this – the reality of a life in which God's life is exposed to the effects of destructive greed, pride and resentment in the human heart, in which we can see how our own urge to defend ourselves can be justified as a defence of God's truth or God's justice. And so part of the truth that the Spirit communicates to us is the knowledge that we're not God. If we think we are, we will end up seeking to exterminate the true God, because we see God as our deadly enemy, our dangerous competitor.

In one way, you could say that the Holy Spirit is given to make us grasp that we are mortal, that we shall die: only when we understand and accept that this is just the way we are can we receive the gift of eternal life as God wants to give it – not the endless prolonging of the life of my precious ego but the endless opening up to be fed by what God freely gives, the depth of loving and mindful joy that we could never invent for ourselves. The great American theologian Stanley Hauerwas likes to quote a Methodist minister who would often begin her sermons by saying 'I could never have thought up the Church'. The gifts of the Spirit, including the gift of each of us to one another, are far in excess of what we thought we needed or could cope with – what we thought we could 'bear'.

Moments when we come face to face with mortality, moments like the time we're still living through, can be moments of grace – not just reminders that we must die and be judged, but moments when I recognize that I don't have to make myself live for ever and that the universe doesn't depend on me personally holding it together and forcing it into shape. The gospel is sceptical about systems of human power because it sees how easily our systems seduce us into thinking that this is our job. The strange fact is that the Spirit fills us with life by acquainting us with death; opens to us a share in the life of God the Holy Trinity by reminding us how very human we are; clothes us with power from on high by entering into the life of our bodies, our frailties and our mistakes, and steadily exposing them to the light of divine love and divine truth.

Not all that easy to bear, then. But the only way to eternal life – which is, as we read in the Gospel of John, knowing the true God and Jesus whom he has sent: the true God who alone can tell us that we're not God, and yet are the infinitely precious and diverse children of God, called to receive gifts without limit and to receive them with and for one another in the unthinkably odd community of the Church.

4 June

Keep yourselves from idols

'Idolatry is ultimately not the worship of things so much as the worship of myself – the reduction of God to the scale of my wants and my comfort.'

The First Letter of St John ends with these words: 'We are in him that is true, even in his Son Jesus Christ. This is the true God, and eternal life. Little children, keep yourselves from idols.' Our identity as Christians is to be in the place where Jesus stands, the place from which we can see into the boundless reality that is the outpouring of God's life. Standing with Jesus, standing in the truth, is like standing under a waterfall: the life of God is around us, soaking and overwhelming us. We can't grab it and hold on to it, we can't contain it. The mystery of the Trinitarian life which we celebrate next Sunday is the mystery of just being immersed in this – the mystery of which baptism is such a fitting sign.

Living in this mystery is the opposite of idolatry, because an idol is precisely something we have made and can manipulate. Idolatry is ultimately not the worship of things so much as the worship of *myself* – the reduction of God to the scale of my wants and my comfort. And it is horribly easy to take even the signs and witnesses of God's truth and turn them into idols in this sense, into things that reinforce who I am or who we are – as a nation, a class, a race.

Quite literally, God alone knows what was going on in the head of the President of the United States as he stood outside a church this week brandishing a Bible, having walked to the church with his path cleared by tear gas and rubber bullets, posturing before a nation more tragically divided than it has been for decades, wounded at so many levels. But objectively this was an act of idolatry – standing somewhere else than in the truth, using the text that witnesses to God's disruptive majesty as a prop in a personal drama. In a context where racial privilege itself has long been an idolatry, where long-unchallenged institutional violence has been a routine means for the defence of that privilege, the image of the President clinging to the Scriptures as if to an amulet is bizarre even by the standards of recent years.

But as we look towards our celebration this coming Sunday, we have to ask about our own faithfulness in standing in the truth, our own idolatries, great and small, as individuals and as a society on this side of the Atlantic. It's easy to focus on that image from Washington as a sign of what's wrong over there; but what do we use to reinforce our own status and comfort? How does the poison of privilege undermine our own integrity?

All of us are in some way touched by idolatry because we all inherit a human condition in which we are in thrall to the fear that we are surrounded by enemies, that we are all either winners or losers, that we have to earn our security at the expense of our fellow humans. And this is the world of untruth from which we are rescued in the baptized life.

So our calling is to go back again and again to stand under the waterfall; to remember that sensation of being unable to measure and contain what surrounds us, and to be reborn in the truth – not so that we can point fingers and judge but so that we can simply declare and show that idolatry in whatever form traps us in a world so much smaller and drier than the real world, the world held eternally in the life of the Father, the Word and the Spirit. 'This is the true God, and eternal life.'

11 June

Corpus Christi

Online communion

'Our common life, in and out of church, depends simply on *what has been done for us*, and in response we can only gaze and adore and give thanks.'

After our service last Sunday, the online discussion turned briefly to people's thoughts about not being able physically to join in the sacrament. A timely reflection for this week: today is traditionally observed as a special festival of the Eucharist, with many churches celebrating it with outdoor processions. In the Middle Ages, it was one of the public high points of the Christian year: in cities in Western Europe, the great medieval miracle plays would be performed in the streets, and there were sometimes great public acts of reconciliation between rival groups or individuals in civic life. It was as if the Eucharist was being affirmed as the true basis of all community, all true public life.

Very different from what we are experiencing today – and yet the strange thing is that in the last couple of months it's not that we have all given up on 'public life'. As a national community, we have taken on board the need to act so as to safeguard the most vulnerable people in the community;

we have learned afresh to be recognize the role of those who quietly keep the common life going; we have been sensitized (a bit) to the realities of hidden privation, emotional strain in domestic circumstances, and the need to be alert both to abuse behind locked doors and to acute loneliness. We haven't retreated into little individual bunkers. And in the last week the global outpouring of grief and anger about injustice and racial violence – even with all the worries about large gatherings from the public health perspective – has at the very least shown us a world whose imagination hasn't grown more selfish or individualistic.

Online worship and the reduced sacramental life it entails have been criticized in some quarters as taking the church out of the public sphere, locking the doors on our calling to transform social life. Whatever the theology, I'm not at all sure that this is what has happened: we could also tell this story as one where quite a lot of people whose exclusion we simply never noticed have been able to share in some way a significant common life as they hear and absorb the pattern of Christian speech, fed by the Word. One friend of mine observed wryly that until we were forced to do it by the medical crisis we as a Church very often simply failed to think hard enough about the needs of rather a lot of people who for one reason or another couldn't get to physical services, with perhaps an occasional clerical visit as the sole point of contact. Now there are new and creative options; we shouldn't see this experience as just a frustrating time of 'making do', but a new opening of doors.

Of course, we all long for the restoring of the possibility of gathering and sharing in the way we are used to – the way we *need* to as material beings. But in this period when we are limited in our access to the material sharing of the sacrament, we can focus on two things. One is simply this fact of having discovered new ways of including people; sharing the liturgy online has become part of the way we relate to a wider 'public' – not by great compelling displays of our national importance, but by patient and imaginative thinking about what makes sense in our local environment and what actually speaks into the need of those around us. Our eyes have been opened a little, our awareness has been woken up.

But the second thing is in some ways harder to say and grasp. The Eucharist is not only an affirmation of the common life we experience in the Holy Spirit, and it is certainly not just a celebration of human togetherness. We look back with puzzlement at the days when – in both Western and Eastern Churches, well into the twentieth century – relatively few people actually took Communion regularly. They went to church to gaze at the drama of God's work of redemption and to adore and give thanks.

This often represented a distorted model of the Eucharist, one that went all too comfortably with a pattern of clerical domination and privilege. Yet, to speak personally for a moment, I have found that the experience of concentrating on 'spiritual communion'; of quieting myself down to focus on the great gift of God in Jesus, absolutely present in this act, these things; of doing all this in the quiet of home, in a moment of physical stillness and silence – all this brings home to me the truth that our common life, in and out of church, depends simply on *what has been done for us*, and in response we can only gaze and adore and give thanks.

Yes of course it isn't the full experience of the Eucharist, and it's one side only of the reality of the sacrament. But if the Eucharist online helps us both to open our eyes more fully to those who are usually excluded and to recognize more gladly and wonderingly the sheer *thereness* of the loving act of God reconciling the world to himself – well, we shall have learned something when we come back physically to the common table and the common meal, something about what 'public life' might really mean. We shall have learned a bit about what those medieval forebears of ours were celebrating in their great Corpus Christi festivities.

18 June

The problem with statues

---

*'Statues, unlike most other artforms, don't tell a story.
Stories allow for change, for failure and success, for the
complexities of people who may be generous and admirable
in some ways and deeply flawed in others.'*

Just opposite the Archbishop's stall in the choir of
Canterbury Cathedral is a monument to a prelate of the
fifteenth century, Archbishop Henry Chichele. On the top
lies his effigy in full vestments; underneath is another effigy
showing him simply as a naked corpse. There are quite a
few such monuments from this period, and some are even
more graphic, showing maggots peeping out from the dead
flesh. The point is one that was familiar in the later Middle
Ages, especially during and after the Black Death: beneath
all human dignity, security and reputation lies the basic fact
of being mortal.

It's really only in the sixteenth century that people's effigies
on tombs begin to show them not as reclining in deathlike
stillness, their hands joined in prayer, but as wakeful, even
active – sometimes resting rather awkwardly on their
elbows, sometimes kneeling upright, and increasingly,
from the mid-seventeenth century, standing, musing or
gesturing, as if alive. Look around in Westminster Abbey

and you'll see what an extraordinary gallery of unlikely poses developed in the eighteenth century, along with longer and more fulsome inscriptions – of the kind that (according to an old anecdote) prompted one Victorian child to ask, 'Why are all the dead people so good?'

From about 1700 onwards, our culture reinvented the habits of the ancient classical world, celebrating wealth and power by erecting statues – not sober or macabre memorials reminding the onlooker of death and judgement, but straightforward affirmations of worldly success. A statue is a very distinct sort of image: it freezes someone in a timeless moment; it literally fixes their position and so in a sense fixes their place in a system of influence and relationships and public mythology.

Which why, I suppose, statues become such a focus for hatred as well as veneration; why we saw giant statues of Saddam Hussein being toppled in Iraq after the war there, and why just at the moment we are seeing such a fierce controversy over statues that in this country and the USA are taken to represent a system of power and wealth that has been built on large-scale exploitation, violence and suppression. I'm not very keen on statues being removed randomly by enthusiastic crowds; and I am very wary of anything that encourages us just to erase bits of our history that we disapprove of. But I understand something of the resentment here. The statue of a slave-trader, with an inscription about his exceptional virtues, isn't something you can argue with: it's *meant* to express solid public approval, the power of social agreement. It's there to help fix or freeze the way a society works and the values it endorses.

Another way of saying this is that statues, unlike most other artforms, don't tell a story. Stories allow for change, for failure and success, for the complexities of people who may be generous and admirable in some ways and deeply flawed in others. Gladstone and Gandhi (to take examples that have been much discussed lately) both began with many views most of us would regard as abhorrent – Gladstone defending slavery, Gandhi expressing his sense of superiority to black people around him in South Africa. Both grew a very long way beyond those early opinions and achieved extraordinary things for oppressed communities. We need the whole story; and a statue never gives you that. Its surface is closed, finished; no room for flaws.

This may be why Eastern Christians don't permit statues of Christ or the saints. Icons, by contrast, are meant to show, not a sealed-off three-dimensional object but a near-transparent surface, a membrane between this world and the deeper world of God's action. They are not portraits but representations of the impact of God upon a human life, with a blaze of foreign light just under the surface of this person's flesh and blood reality. And with images of the saints, this helps us see them as depictions of lives that are not finished and enclosed but lives in the process of being constantly re-made by God. There is a sort of *mobility* in these images. Where images of Christ are concerned, we're looking at a reality where this human form is the source of the light that makes sense and shape of the rest of the world. In icons of the Transfiguration especially, you can often trace the direction of the rays of light and see that their geometric point of convergence is in the centre of the figure of Jesus. How could you capture that in a three-dimensional image that you could walk around?

So I find myself sensing a fair bit of sympathy with the feelings of those who want to see the polished and smooth images of outrageous injustice taken from their pedestals. To be honest, I don't much like statues at the best of times; there is something uncomfortably self-satisfied about so many of them. But before we set out on a spree of destruction directed at the images of those who fail to live up to our impeccable contemporary moral standards, we should remember that these are images of people like us, who got many things wrong and perhaps a few things right; whose human reality wasn't a finished work of art but a mortal and messy business, ending in death but open to grace.

What matters is that we keep on telling the story, and learning to *re-tell* it – making room for the voices we have silenced, thinking again about the patterns of power we have taken for granted, understanding that our flaws and sins mean that we shall never stop re-learning and re-making the history of our world and our lives within it. Under the surface of power lies fragility and mortality; under the reality of mortality and failure lies the light of grace. When we have stopped arguing about the rights and wrongs of statues, we still have to build the relations of justice, truthfulness and compassion that will allow us to be both judged and renewed by that light.

25 June
Second nature

'Over time we grow and change; habits that once seemed 'natural' come to seem strange. New things, new perspectives, are taken for granted.'

News this week of the relaxing of social distancing regulations has been met with what Gilbert and Sullivan's *Mikado* memorably described as 'modified rapture'. If we're honest, what most of us would really like is a clear declaration that we can now stop thinking and worrying all the time about our behaviour in public and get back to being unselfconscious. And we're obviously not quite there yet.

Whether in what we say or what we do, it's a nuisance feeling that we have to keep a close watch on ourselves – pulling ourselves up, watching out for pitfalls. When grumpy columnists in the press mutter, 'You can't say anything these days' – meaning that casual expressions of prejudice or demeaning stereotypes are more likely to be challenged than they used to be – they are giving voice to something we can all understand, even those of us who try very hard to be more aware. It's not always easy remembering to avoid certain ways of talking, just as it's hard work to remember rules about social distance, or how many people you're supposed to be talking to or eating with.

Yet over time we grow and change; habits that once seemed 'natural' come to seem strange. New things, new perspectives, are taken for granted. I wonder whether we'll come to think of this period of more careful or self-aware ways of moving round and touching one another in a time of infectious disease as a bit like the development of the old 'Highway Code' – learning and internalising a set of new habits that will keep us all safer in a changed world. After a while, these habits stop being self-conscious because we recognize that they 'hang together', they make sense as a set of social practices that bring us closer and help us trust one another.

St Paul tells us to be 'transformed by the renewing of our minds' (Romans 12.2). And in the discussion that follows in his letter to the Romans, he makes clear that this is essentially about learning the habits that will create trust, minimize resentment and rivalry, and dissolve our greedy longing to occupy the high ground at our neighbour's expense. Transformation is the process of growing into a state in which this is second nature to us – a state in which we are so deeply attentive to the practical and psychological needs of those around us, so unfussed about our own status, so liberated from the longing to save and solve everything by our own wisdom and heroism, that we instinctively speak and act in ways that give life to the neighbour. This, for Paul, is what it is to live in Christ and to let Christ live in us – the Christ who is uniquely, freely and eternally attentive to the world's needs at every level.

Growing into this is a long and frankly painful business. As I write, I think of the Collect for the Feast of the Nativity of St John the Baptist, the prayer that we may 'patiently suffer for the truth's sake'. It rings a bell here. The truth is God's eternal purpose for a loving, joyful, mutually nourishing human world; what we so regularly take for granted may feel obvious to us; but if it implies carelessness of the life or dignity or human worth of anyone else, it embodies a deep untruthfulness. Transformation starts with looking – gratefully, prayerfully, quietly – into the truth as Christ uncovers it to us. Absorbing it into our very DNA, so to speak, is slow going. But we can look at those for whom this attentive generosity has indeed become second nature, and hope and pray that we too can become naturally, unselfconsciously aware of what the neighbour needs, and adjust our own lives around that without resentment – perhaps even, in the long run, with unmodified rapture.

2 July
Meditative walking

'In meditative walking we trace over the world's surface the path to God; we affirm that whatever steps we take can be part of our journey home to the source of all things, in Jesus who is the Way.'

In the process of trying to clear out my bookshelves, prior to our impending house move, all sorts of things, not surprisingly, have come to light. One in particular seems worth sharing at this moment when we're just beginning to think we might be able to be physically back in church before too long.

About eighteen months ago, I went to Sweden to take part in a conference. My kind hosts drove me through a snow-covered landscape to have a meal in the city of Linköping. On the way to the conference centre they asked whether I'd ever heard of Bishop Martin Lonnebo – which I hadn't. He's still alive, now over 90, and has had an enormous spiritual influence in Sweden, especially when he was bishop of Linköping in the 1980's. His most visible legacy, though, is from just after his retirement, when he devised a simple form of meditation with prayer beads, called the 'Pearls of Life'. The wonderful medieval cathedral in Linköping has translated this into a guided walk around the building, with small semi-precious stones set into the floor at intervals where you can stop and reflect – a *via sacra*, a sacred journey through the building.

It begins with the 'pearl of God' – the simple recognition that God is both infinite and intimate and always bestowing light. And then there is the 'I-pearl' – standing for the 'nothingness penetrated by everything' that is you and me. The journey continues, to pearls representing baptism, silence, desert, deeper silence, love, mystery, night, dawn and resurrection. Each 'station' has a short text to reflect on, from the Bible or from the Swedish hymn book, and some words of encouragement. At the 'Love Pearl', otherwise called 'God's Heart', the text reads:

The cross is a sign of the deepest love in the universe.
The four winds of heaven meet here.
This is where the Tree of Life is replanted;
It provides blessed fruit.
The cross follows us from birth, to death, into eternity.
Through baptism we are marked with the sign of Life.
The breaking of the bread shows us how life should be.

My attempt to clear up my study had uncovered the little booklet I'd been given on my visit to the cathedral. It made me think about our own church, and about the fact that the restored and cleaned Stations of the Cross are back in the building, and about how significant it is when somehow we can connect the building with the rhythms of our personal prayers. Meditative walking is a very old tradition, in Christianity and in other traditions too. We can make the church building more significant for ourselves by walking meditatively around it – and so long as access is restricted, as it is at the moment, one person walking round may have extra opportunities for reflection. And we can reproduce this sacred journey in our own homes or gardens, using one or other form of the circlet of beads that Christians have used for centuries: the rosary, the Greek 'prayer rope', Bishop Lonnebo's 'pearls'...

In meditative walking we trace over the world's surface the path to God; we affirm that whatever steps we take can be part of our journey home to the source of all things, in Jesus who is 'the Way'. We can do this at home and find that our pilgrimage is a matter of doing the most ordinary and everyday things. We can make a literal pilgrimage to a shrine and see it as a symbol of the upheavals and new beginnings in which our life in the new creation unfolds. We can make the spaces of our own church buildings speak and sing by slow, loving pacing around them.

Whether it's the Stations of the Cross or the labyrinth, or some other form of Christian journey, it's important that our churches breathe the invitation to prayerful journeying. They're not just convenient buildings to have services in; they are spaces open for our discovery of God, helping us to see all space, every place as a centre for God's loving presence.

The journey in Linköping ends with these words:

The rest of the walk on the Path of Reverence for Life brings you deeper into your earthly calling, as well as into the endless depths of God's mercy.

9 July

Power to be free

'We long for freedom from constraint so that there
will be more space for active love. And we resist
arbitrary power because it stifles that love.'

Earlier this week, the Church of England calendar
commemorated Thomas More and John Fisher – two
people who you might say died in order to stop the Church
of England coming into existence. Both were executed
by Henry VIII for refusing to sign up to his agenda of
subordinating the Church completely to his own royal
authority, and for refusing to sanction his second marriage.
They were not heroes of individual conscience in the
modern sense, as they both believed firmly in a supernatural
revelation that had absolute claims on all human beings.
Thomas More in his day had executed heretics without a
second thought.

So why exactly should we celebrate them, alongside those
who died under Henry's daughter Mary for their refusal to
accept the authority of the Pope? Surely they wouldn't thank
us for it! Are we just reducing these figures to examples of
generic bravery in witnessing to their faith – never mind
what that faith was?

There's a bit more to it than that. It's sometimes been said that 'heretics' are right in what they affirm and wrong in what they deny. This amounts to saying that those whom the Church defines as outside the bounds of authentic teaching are at least trying to advance *some* aspect of the Christian faith, and it's a pity that they can't see that other ways of speaking witness to exactly what they want to say themselves.

Yes, fair enough. But I'm tempted to turn this upside down when I look at the struggles and sufferings of the Reformation era, and say that often people are right in what they *deny*. Thomas More and John Fisher wanted to deny that a ruler or government had control over the Church in such a way that no one had the freedom to challenge the sovereign power. Cranmer and his fellow-Reformers wanted to deny that the hierarchical system of the Church of the Middle Ages could ignore the criticisms that would arise when it was set alongside the witness of the New Testament. What they were *all* denying was power that could never be questioned.

And, of course, that also meant that they affirmed some things that were just as problematic. More and Fisher believed the only defence against arbitrary use of royal power was an all-powerful Church hierarchy. The Reformers in England believed the only defence against the tyranny of the papacy was an all-powerful king.

So, what if both those affirmations were wrong? What if denying arbitrary top-down power in one area means you have to resist it in every other area it operates? 'Power' in the New Testament is almost always to do with the freedom to release, to heal, to forgive – or, as in the wonderful phrase in the first chapter of John's Gospel, 'power [or 'authority'] to become children of God.' This form of power is an *absence of constraint* – not a way of putting constraints on everyone else. Our current experience of slowly emerging (for now, anyway) from lockdown gives us a vivid sense of what it's like to have constraints lifted, and to feel we can actually move and develop and explore. We accept constraints for good reason – such as we have certainly had in recent months. But we have quite rightly also been arguing about this, hoping for something better, working together to make more real freedom possible in the long term – the freedom to release and heal. We long for freedom from constraint so that there will be more space for active love. And we resist arbitrary power because it stifles that love.

More, Fisher, Cranmer, Tyndale, all the martyrs on both sides of the Reformation, died because they felt compelled to resist the claims of naked power, and believed with all their hearts that the power they denied was an enemy to the free love of God and to the transforming grace that would re-create us in God's image. Celebrating Christians who died on opposing sides of a great and tragic controversy may look odd – or perhaps just a bit of typical Anglican hedging our bets. But what we celebrate is the intensity of a faith that makes it clear what you must deny: which is all kinds of power that are too fearful and (in the long run) too *weak* to face challenge.

The truest human power is –as Russell Hoban puts it in his extraordinary novel about post-nuclear Britain, *Riddley Walker* – the freedom to 'get out of the way', so that the healing and releasing act of God can come through. And in some way every true martyr's death is about that. Even the austere Thomas More on the scaffold prayed that he and his killers might yet 'merrily meet in heaven'; he died with the hope of healing in his eyes.

16 July

Behind the mask

'We talk a lot about "the face we present to the world", about "saving face" or "losing face", about "putting a brave face on things" – and so much of this kind of language suggests that our 'face' is something we can work on and polish until it shows only what we want to show.'

Part of my leisure reading in the last couple of weeks has been one of the three very large volumes of C. S. Lewis's collected letters. This week I've been reading some of what Lewis wrote about the composition of his final novel, *Till We Have Faces*.

It's a book quite unlike anything else he ever wrote, a long retelling of the old Greek story of Eros and Psyche – the story of how the beautiful Psyche (the Greek for 'soul') is captivated by Eros (divine love), and how, after she is tricked by her jealous sisters into betraying Eros, she has to struggle and suffer to find him again and be reconciled. The tale is an obvious allegory; but what Lewis does with it is to turn it into a compelling story that still has immense spiritual resonance but is also a credible and moving narrative. And he chooses to tell it through the eyes of Psyche's sister; it's the only story he ever wrote from a woman's point of view, and it should make anyone who sees Lewis as just an old-style misogynist think again.

I shan't try to summarize it. The point that seemed suddenly relevant this week was Lewis's argument with his publisher over the title. Lewis wanted to call it *Bareface*; the publisher didn't like this at all, and Lewis finally and reluctantly agreed to change it to the title we know. He wanted to call it *Bareface* because its real theme is how we keep on refusing to recognize who and what we truly are. If we – like the sister who narrates the story – both mock and envy those who are touched by the frightening strangeness of divine love, is it in fact because we simply don't know what we most deeply want and need? And if we don't know ourselves, how can we know God in his truth? How can we look him in the face 'till we have faces'?

We talk a lot about 'the face we present to the world', about 'saving face ' or 'losing face', about 'putting a brave face on things' – and so much of this kind of language suggests that our 'face' is something we can work on and polish until it shows only what we want to show. We don't want our faces to 'betray' us. But when we turn to God (to borrow one of St Paul's most striking images) 'the veil is removed'; we can't put on any kind of face for him, we are left naked to his gaze. If we can gradually get used to the painful recognition involved in this, the recognition of our humiliating fondness for fairy tales about what we are really like, we can turn also to each other and get used to a higher degree of honesty and mutual understanding.

The question of using face masks in the present health crisis seems to touch many people on the raw. Whereas relatively few in this country adopt the daft response of saying, 'No one's going to tell *me* what to do', rather more of us feel very uncomfortable with having to mask our faces. How do we properly 'read' someone else's expression? How do we present *ourselves* in the best way possible if our faces are hidden?

Yes, wearing masks makes us feel awkward and a bit disadvantaged. But I also think that it just might make us pay more attention to the *whole* of how someone else is behaving or communicating. I can remember the experience of lecturing in Muslim institutions with a lot of veiled women in the audience, and getting used after a while to paying attention to eye movements, hand movements and the like, and realising that I was picking up many of the communicative signs that I would otherwise pick up by looking at faces. I began to be able to tell if they were bored or interested, sympathetic or suspicious. And we all know that in any conversation we look and listen to far more than words or facial expressions.

Wearing face masks can remind us of just how varied and surprising a thing human communication is; and it can remind us also of the strange fact that wearing a mask may make us *more* not less vulnerable to one another – in the sense that we don't quite know how much we may be 'giving away' if we can't give clear expression to our feelings by the expressions we put on our faces.

Perhaps we are more 'barefaced' sometimes when we wear masks. When we turn to God we have to take away the veils – that is, we have to let go of the ways we control our public image, the image that saves face or loses face, that puts on a face for the world. In God's presence, it's our whole body, our whole self that speaks to God – in silence, in kneeling or prostration, in lifting hands and eyes. It's as we attend to the wholeness of each other's bodily presence, and as we hold our bodies restfully and alertly in God's presence while we worship that we begin slowly to grow towards the freedom to put aside our home-made, self-serving masks – to grow 'till we have faces'.

23 July

At home in the world

'Underneath what we feel about all the things on which
we sometimes get fixated there lies a basic human longing
to be 'at home' with what truly is – with one another,
with our Maker, with the raw stuff of the world.'

Wednesday's news announced the discovery of new
archaeological material suggesting that the presence of
homo sapiens in America went back many thousands
of years before the estimate previously advanced by the
experts. Even though there hasn't yet been any clear DNA
evidence from the site in question, they've found a few
things that can only be the product of deliberate, intelligent
work – basic tools which tell us that those who lived
there were able to work out techniques of changing their
environment, making themselves a little more at home in
the world they inhabited.

It's quite a significant point that what helps us recognize
the signs of human presence is seeing the trace of activities
by which someone is *making a difference*. And it ought to
remind us that the worst thing we can do to other human
beings is to frustrate their freedom to make a difference –
their freedom to work on the raw material of the world and
become more at home there. One theologian I read years

ago said that it's all to do with the process by which the world we belonged to became the world that belonged to us.

On its own, though, that's a rather ambiguous way of putting it – as if the world could ever 'belong' to us as humans, as if we didn't really belong in and to our environment. But this theologian went on to say that he thought *gardening* was one of the best metaphors for this process. And gardening only works if you start by really learning the ins and outs of the world you belong to, finding out what the natural rhythms of things are, and working with the grain of things to bring about something that is both 'natural' and new. Only if you begin from that level of quiet attention, really learning the 'feel' of soil and plant life and weather, can you actually make the sort of difference that lasts. We've all heard the horror stories of projects that have failed because no one bothered to work out the balance of a natural environment before introducing some new element that threatened the whole ecology of a region (remember the disaster of introducing cane toads into Australia).

It's even more complicated when what we are trying to change is the behaviour of our fellow human beings. In the last months, we have had to think a lot about what sort of messages, incentives, threats and promises will alter human behaviour in times of crisis. People in leadership positions have flailed around rather in this respect – not all that surprisingly, of course, given that the challenge has been on such a scale. Yet in one way or another, we all spend a lot of time trying to change on another. We want to persuade others to think like us; we want to get them to see things our way and behave in ways that won't threaten themselves or us; we want to nudge them this way or that so that we can all feel more at home. And quite often it looks as though we have learned very little about this since the days of our cave-dwelling ancestors.

One way of looking at this is to recognize that what really shifts our behaviour is a belief that the goal we are offered is something we will love because it promises us joy. We can trivialize this, as the advertiser and the sloganeering politician do. But it doesn't change the fact that we act because we *want*. To be human is to desire; we work, we make things, we produce both art and science because we desire more freedom, more harmony, more of a sense of being at home in the world.

Our Christian faith doesn't tell us that we shouldn't want or long for anything, that desire is evil. It does tell us, though, that any kind of wanting that is at odds with the grain of what's actually there, whether in the material world or in the lives of other human beings, is doomed – and finally self-destructive. We have to learn that underneath what we feel about all the things on which we sometimes get fixated there lies a basic human longing to be 'at home' with what truly is – with one another, with our Maker, with the raw stuff of the world. In the terms used by many early Christian theologians, we have to learn about the 'logos' that unites us – the eternal energy of God in sharing life and making harmony. It is an everlasting reality in God's life, and it is also what God shares with creation (as the beginning of St John's Gospel makes clear).

And it is what comes fully to life in the world in Jesus.

What he does in the cross and the resurrection and the giving of the Spirit is to open our eyes and transform our hearts so that we can see just a bit of what it might be to see our own longings as bound up with the joy and fulfilment of every other part of creation. When our eyes are open like that, we can understand better what sort of work we are called to do and what sort of tools we need – work that grows out of the patience to search for a vision that all can recognize as life-giving tools that fit into a human hand and 'know' how to find their way to the place where they have the simplest and best leverage.

When it came to the way they worked and how they used their tools, it looks as though our cave-dwelling ancestors knew a thing or two. God save us from the snobbery of condescending to the 'primitive'! What so often moves us about the remains of earliest humanity is the sense that they cared about how to live together in security, to discover meaning and develop deeper communication – to live by 'logos', just as we strive to do today as part of Christ's Body.

30 July

Liturgy in life

'Making homes and food, making events, making music, making safety and provision for one another, all of this is the "liturgy" in which God calls us to take part.'

We can only cope with so many issues at a time, I know; but sometimes it's important to try and remember the things that the media are not currently putting before us, and not just to think about what's catching the headlines.

This came home to me at a meeting this week to discuss and hear about plans for a major international initiative next year to bring the plight of child refugees back into the public eye. The big challenges are the same as ever – guaranteeing safe and legal transit for under-age youngsters to a secure environment. But the extra problem of the extreme vulnerability of overcrowded refugee facilities to pandemic disease ought to be concentrating our minds rather more urgently at the moment.

You'll hear more details in due course, but this is what is planned in outline. A series of small groups will be escorting a twelve-foot puppet on foot from the border of Syria to the UK, via Turkey, Greece, Italy, Switzerland, Belgium, Germany and France, ending up in Manchester. The puppet represents a nine-year-old girl. At every stage of the journey, there will be events to welcome 'Amal', the refugee girl, and to highlight the human tragedies she represents. It's a wonderfully imaginative project, and one of its designers said at the meeting that he wants this to be a proof of his confidence that 'when people see beauty they become better'.

It's a wonderful slogan; even though I suspect the real problem is getting people to stop shouting and competing and obsessing long enough to see the beauty in the first place. But the other insight that stuck with me was a comment from another of the designers. In the activities around the journey, she said, we want to involve people from every kind of social background because when people are engaged in *making* something together – whether it's a very concrete thing, a building or a meal, or a celebration, a play or a musical performance – they forget the baggage they bring with them and find a shared joy and a fresh identity.

Well, the project is a really exciting one, and I have high hopes. It's being organized by 'Good Chance', a theatre group who put on that amazing drama in London a couple of years ago, *The Jungle*, a play about the experience of the notorious camp near Calais, with many actual refugees among the actors. An unforgettable event; look up their website for more about them (and how to donate!). But this point about working together struck a chord especially for today, which is the day in the Church of England calendar when we remember the first generation of activists who campaigned against the slave trade: Equiano, Clarkson and Wilberforce.

One of the simplest things we can say about the dreadful and inhuman perversity of slavery is that it's the opposite of working *together*. Slave and slave-owner don't share in a common task; they have no opportunity of forgetting their difference in a single collaborative project where all make their contribution, shape the outcome, recognize each other's skill and resourcefulness. One person simply tells the other what they want and the other has to do it.

It helps from time to time to remember that the word 'liturgy' which we use for our formal worship actually means 'the people's work' – quite literally something we make together, in the unity of Christ's Body. We're not slaves, says Jesus in John's Gospel, because slaves don't know what's going on in the master's mind; we're called to be friends together, bound by one project in which we all have a distinctive share. The great twentieth-century Russian saint and martyr, Mother Maria Skobtsova, used to like to talk about how the liturgy – so to speak – leaked out of the church door, inseparable from the common work, the shared making, that we should be engaged with in every area of our lives.

That project is the life of the Kingdom – the community God wants to see on earth, where no one is forgotten or disposable, and all are invited to the ongoing work. Making homes and food, making events, making music, making safety and provision for one another, all of this is the 'liturgy' in which God calls us to take part – and the liturgy of our worship together is both the springboard for this and the place where we see it in its fullest and most joyful context.

I like the thought of 'Amal''s walk next year as a journey that illuminates what we mean by liturgy – calling us back to recognize how easily we settle with slavery for ourselves and for others, and to see the beauty and the hope that common work brings. May we all learn to worship in that Spirit and that truth.

6 August
Transfiguration

'The apostles Peter, James and John saw what a human face could be. They knew that humanity could be the face worn by God. And whatever terrors, crimes and catastrophes might follow, nothing could extinguish that eternal light.'

Seventy-five years ago today the atom bomb was dropped on Hiroshima. Most of us have grown up with the abstract possibility of nuclear warfare in the back of our minds, and we can only imagine how shocking it must have been when this massive destructive potential was first made manifest.

And yet, looking back at 1945, what is surprising is how relatively few people immediately recognized that something fundamental had changed in the moral climate; the majority seemed not to notice that anything that shocking had happened. Perhaps we had become hardened to shock as the Second World War unfolded – and especially as the nightmares of the German concentration camps were revealed.

But some were shocked and recognized that a boundary had been crossed. One of them was the Roman Catholic scholar Ronald Knox, who, in the autumn of 1945, wrote a short book called *God and the Atom*, trying to express his sense that something had happened which struck at the heart of faith, hope and charity alike. In the dropping of the bomb we had pushed our own arbitrary and greedy human will so far into the depths of the material world that nothing now seemed to be safe from our murderous ambition for control.

One of Knox's chapters is entitled, 'A Missed Opportunity'. What if, he says, we had found it possible to demonstrate the hideousness of this weapon in a remote place and then said, 'And that is why we can't and shan't use it'? Yes, we are all affected by the adrenaline rush of violent conflict: 'To fight with the gloves off may be an invigorating experience while the actual crisis lasts.' But Knox goes on to say that this will leave a foul taste in the long run. We have tasted the worst of ourselves; we have had to look at the vilest we are capable of – mass murder by technological skill. And we will probably then either put enormous energy into denying this (and blaming others) or adopt a negative and cynical approach to our shared humanity, in which everything comes down to competitions for power.

It's hard to quarrel with the implication that the advent of the nuclear age has introduced higher levels of both denial and cynicism into our public life and our expectations of humanity; we don't have far to look for examples. But Knox steers us towards the key point here. We are capable of horrors – Belsen, Auschwitz, Hiroshima and Nagasaki, Rwanda and Srebrenica. But we see these as horrors precisely because we know that not one of them was forced on us, not one of them was inevitable. We chose. And to say we made a dreadful choice is also to know that there were other choices that were possible. We are not *doomed* to evil. The problem is that we are seduced by it, reassured by it, fascinated by it, and all too ready to gloss over it and justify it when it suits us. It's not that we need to be liberated from an iron necessity. It's tougher than that: we need to be liberated from an addiction that we always seem to be eager either to deny or to rationalize. We can't see straight or think straight.

It's one of the greatest ironies that today is also the Feast of Christ's Transfiguration – that strange story of how the three favoured apostles saw blinding light streaming from the face and figure of Jesus as they prayed with him on the misty peak of a mountain, wrapped up in a choking fog of glory. They heard a voice simply saying 'Listen to Jesus'; they somehow picked up that he was speaking with Moses and Elijah, those other mountaintop visionaries, about his coming journey to Jerusalem, to humiliation and death. They were granted briefly to see the unbearable radiance of presence and action that streams eternally from God – and to see it in the travel-stained, dishevelled humanity of their friend and teacher. They saw a human face and understood that behind and beyond it was infinite love and beauty – so that when, later on, they looked on that face disfigured and bleeding they should not forget the brightness of the mystery that shone through it.

The apostles Peter, James and John saw what a human face could be. They knew that humanity could be the face worn by God. And whatever terrors, crimes and catastrophes might follow, nothing could extinguish that eternal light. Humans remain free to turn back to that light; to do so they need all the love and grace that Christ's life and death and resurrection and Spirit can give, but it is never impossible. We can turn from greedy self-interest, we can say no to the glamour of violence and domination, we can listen to God's Son and follow his way of hope-full vulnerability. Rare certainly, elusive and unpredictable, but real. 'The Saint', says Knox, 'holds, like the atom, strange forces hidden under a mask of littleness.'

13 August

To be born again

'What if the point of all we achieve, all we succeed in,
is to teach us to *receive* more deeply and peacefully?
As if what we need to produce by the time of our death
is just – child-like simplicity?'

The feast day that's coming up this Saturday commemorates the end of the earthly life of the Virgin Mary. It's a feast that's celebrated in both Eastern and Western Christianity. By the fifth or sixth century, legends had developed of Mary being taken directly into heaven at her death, like Elijah in the Old Testament; and as the Middle Ages went on, the belief that she never actually died had become very widespread in the West. In 1950, Pope Pius XII (while not endorsing the legendary elements of the tradition) declared that it was an essential part of Christian faith to believe that she had indeed been 'assumed' into heaven. The Western Church has long celebrated this as the feast of Mary's 'Assumption'.

Anglicans have been a bit cautious about taking all of this on board. Fair enough to celebrate the end of Mary's earthly life, even to say that she must surely have been taken at once into the joy of her Risen Son. But the later folklore is less easy to digest.

Interestingly, the Eastern Church has always seen the feast a bit differently. It's called 'the Falling-Asleep of the Mother of God' in the East, or the 'Dormition'. The icons that depict this event are very distinctive, and quite unlike the extravagant pictures in the West of Mary ascending in clouds and being crowned by her Son. In these Eastern icons, Mary lies on her deathbed, surrounded by the apostles – and next to her bed stands Jesus, holding in his arms what looks like a tightly swaddled child. This is Mary's soul, which he is receiving into its rest. It's a poignant turning around of the familiar image of Mary hugging the infant Jesus; here is the Son embracing his mother's 'new-born' life. Because that is what has happened: Mary has begun her life afresh in the closer company of Jesus.

Sometimes when famous people are interviewed, they are asked how they want to be remembered; they are invited to think of the achievements they would like to have piled up by the end of their lives, as if the goal of life were to arrive at a condition of maturity and control, of wise and powerful action. Yet here is Mary at the end of her life and the beginning of her new life, a helpless child again. She can say and do nothing, and she doesn't have to; she is simply welcomed by Christ's love. She doesn't need a monument recording her triumphs, she doesn't have to present her proud credentials at the gate of heaven. Like the Psalmist (Ps.131), she can say, 'My soul is even as a weaned child.'

What if this is really the purpose of our lives? What if the point of all we achieve, all we succeed in, is to teach us to *receive* more deeply and peacefully? As if what we need to produce by the time of our death is just – child-like simplicity? Being able at last just to be welcomed, to be embraced by the Real that we've so long neglected and even run away from? Whatever life is like on the far side of death, it's a reasonable guess that it is not like anything we could have imagined. It *could not be* another episode in the great drama of Myself, my busy, worried, ambitious, talkative, fearful self.

The Orthodox icon of Mary's dormition presents a challenging image of Jesus' words in the Gospels about becoming children again if we are to enter the Kingdom. It reminds us also of the verse in St Peter's first Letter, where he tells his readers (possibly candidates waiting for baptism) that they must be like new-born children, eager to be fed by the living Truth.

As usual, it's a huge paradox. We do indeed have to grow, to make mistakes, to love and be loved, to risk hurting and being hurt in our tangled lives; we need to develop our imagination and intellect, and to battle against all those systems by which some human beings try to keep others in 'infantile' subjection or degradation. (Remember all those people who used to think that the non-European 'races' were somehow like children, needing our wise grown-up guidance and discipline?) And yet, the point of it all, of all the struggle and painful growing and learning, is that we have the space, the freedom and the joy to become simple again, to be like children, able to receive, to be embraced.

If I had to make a personal choice of the two greatest poems in English about heaven, I'd go for George Herbert's 'Love' and Charles Causley's 'Eden Rock'. Herbert imagines arguing with God that he doesn't deserve to be there; God shrugs (as it were) and says 'You must sit down... and taste my meat'; and the poet ends, with those bare monosyllables, 'So I did sit and eat.' Causley imagines seeing his long-dead parents on the other side of a river, setting out a picnic and beckoning him across, reassuring him that it is not difficult. The poem ends with another string of stunned, simple monosyllables: 'I had not thought that it would be like this.'

And that perhaps is the song the Virgin sang as she was embraced by her Son in death.

20 August

The rule of the algorithm

'It's as though each of us is silently being measured
against a mathematical average or a statistical probability. All
those hidden things that actually make us who we are, the
unimaginably complex cocktail of forces that inform
our choices and preferences and actions, are simply
screened out.'

It's been a roller-coaster week for Britain's school-leavers,
and it isn't over yet, alas. A lot could be said about the casual
insensitivity of the government's handling of students'
exam results and the contempt it implies for the educational
process. Why – we might well ask – did it ever seem a
defensible idea that students' efforts should be assessed by
statistical predictions rather than actual performance? We
know that exams are certainly not a watertight means of
assessment, given the effects of exam-related stress on so
many young people, but at least they have something to do
with work done by a human being in a particular time and
place.

As some commentators have begun to notice, it's not
just a problem with educational assessment. As we've noted
before, the rule of the algorithm seems to be omnipresent,
and here to stay. It's bound up with our awed reverence for

what digital mechanisms can now achieve, the processing and analysis of quantities of statistical information that would take the human brain vastly longer to deal with. Most of us are familiar with the way targeted advertisements pop up on our screens – all based on this unimaginable capacity to organize data. 'People who bought this also bought....' Our history of choice is trawled through and we are triumphantly told what we are now likely to want.

Happily, many of us are just about counter-suggestible enough to ignore such suggestions simply because we're told they're so likely. (Sheer bloody-mindedness is a substantial argument for human free-will at the end of the day!) But so much of what we're presented with is more subtle and insidious. It's as though each of us is silently being measured against a mathematical average or a statistical probability. All those hidden things that actually make us who we are, the unimaginably complex cocktail of forces that inform our choices and preferences and actions, are simply screened out.

Whether we notice it or not, we are part of a culture in which information overload leads to the cultivation of ignorance. It sounds a bit odd put like that, but the fact is that any system dealing with huge amounts of input has to select, and thus to *ignore* a proportion of what's flooding in. There's a good case for thinking that the 'modern' human being has lost various sensory skills that would have been active a few thousand years ago. Even today, we can still just about see in some human populations like the San in Southern Africa evidence of kinds of attunement to environmental stimuli that we just don't have any longer.

The dangerous and disturbing thing about our present situation, though, is that we end up not simply failing to notice things about our overall physical environment (bad enough, in all conscience) but failing to see the distinctiveness and mysteriousness of human agents. When we speak about seeing the 'image of God' in human beings, we don't (or we shouldn't!) mean that in certain respects like freedom and intelligence human beings are 'quite like' God. It's more that when I really look at another human being I'm faced with something so different from me and so unfathomable that it's like looking into the unfathomable and endless mystery of God. I can't own it, I can't predict its future, I can't reproduce its inner workings.

It's the very opposite of 'algorithm' thinking. It's tied up with the revolutionary biblical idea that everyone has an unrepeatable gift to give to the community of God's children; and with the rather stunning biblical image of a God who 'calls the stars by name' – a God who is completely committed to a unique relationship with every being that has been created. This is the God who is a loving and patient witness to the whole of the history of each one of us – who, in St Augustine's phrase, is always at home in us, even when we are far away from ourselves and from reality.

A really human and humane education – let alone a Christian education – should be turning our minds and imaginations back to this dimension of wonder at the unfathomable *differences* of which the world is composed. It's all the more shabby and scandalous that anyone should think we can deal with educational discernment by means of statistical calculation; and all the more necessary for communities of faith to hold on stubbornly to that conviction about the divine image – what a modern Russian saint called the 'terror' of the mystery in the face of the neighbour, which is also the doorway into the terrible and glorious mystery of God.

27 August
Praying for Jerusalem

'What we need is the rekindling of *desire* – the sheer passionate longing to see a social order at which the Holy Lamb of God might look without heartbreak. Arrows of desire; the courage and endurance of mental fight; the struggle to keep this imagination alive and burning – this is what we pray for.'

The week's shock/horror story seems to have been the revelation that the BBC were supposedly considering removing 'Rule, Britannia!' from *The Last Night of the Proms*. Our very un-ritualistic society is pretty passionate about the few corporate rituals it has left, and the very thought of changing what is in fact a rather recent tradition was a heaven-sent gift for alarmist media outlets. It was even deemed serious enough for the Prime Minister to make a comment.

I suppose it's understandable that many of us feel the need for something positive about our country as we come to terms with a lot of uncomfortable statistics around our handling of the pandemic. No one has been particularly reassured by the various claims for our 'world-beating' systems. (And why, for goodness' sake, must we talk about 'world-beating', as if effective response to a global crisis were another cheap winner-takes-all competition between rivals?) It seems a harsh blow to be deprived of an evening of unreflective celebration of the national heritage.

Confession time: I rather like 'Rule, Britannia!', in much the same way that I like Gilbert and Sullivan. It's exuberant and magnificently silly and full of irresistible gusto; given the chance, I'll cheerfully join in. But it does no harm to stop and ask a bit about unintended consequences if we make this a central item in a showcase of national pride. The eighteenth century patriots who first wrote and sang that 'Britons never shall be slaves' were intensely relaxed, as they say, about quite a lot of other people being slaves, and it's become that little bit harder to forget this.

I'd be more worried if we dropped 'Jerusalem', to be honest. It's rather a mystery why this strange lyric should have captured the hearts of so many (though Parry's wonderful melody helps). It's part of the introduction to a typically idiosyncratic sequence of poems by England's greatest radical poet, William Blake, alluding to the myth that the young Jesus visited Britain. What if 'the Countenance Divine' actually beheld the realities of Britain, then and now?

No one is sure what Blake meant by mentioning 'dark, Satanic mills' as part of what Jesus would have seen and moved among, but the candidates include early industrial sites, Druidic temples and (I'm afraid) Anglican parish churches. The point, though, is that we are being asked to *imagine* that the incarnate God moved and worked even in the middle of the cruelty, hypocrisy and exploitation that are an inseparable part of every human community's history. 'Jerusalem' is being built, even while all the signs in society around us seem to negate the vision.

What we need is the rekindling of *desire* – the sheer passionate longing to see a social order at which the Holy Lamb of God might look without heartbreak. Arrows of desire; the courage and endurance of mental fight; the struggle to keep this imagination alive and burning – this is what we pray for. The poem looks back to an imaginary past and forward to an imagined future, but at its heart is the question: 'do you truly *want* to live in Jerusalem? Because if you do, you need to remember that it is always already here and now; because even where justice and love seem to be defeated, the Holy Lamb of God is present.'

St Augustine said that societies were unified by what they desired; we have a problem when the wants of a community are so diverse and fragmented that we lose any sense of goals and visions that we can own together. And the Church is united not by any institutional framework as such but by the urge and the *urgency* of the Holy Spirit making us hungry and thirsty for God's justice and compassion to prevail on earth. When we recognize our desire, we also recognize what we *lack*; we celebrate not what we've got or what we've achieved but what we long for, with joyful anticipation. In our worship, above all in the Eucharist, we are given a foretaste of what will finally satisfy our hunger, as the urgent pleading of the Spirit in us meets and is answered by the urgent invitation and the unreserved gift of Christ.

So when we sing 'Jerusalem', we acknowledge something far deeper than the jolly self-satisfaction of 'Rule, Britannia!' We acknowledge that the hills are 'clouded', that the Satanic mills still work at full blast; we can't look at our society, our world, our history with complacency, with nationalist smugness or empty optimism. But there *is* something that makes us long for Jerusalem, the dwelling of God with humans, even if we don't use those words. The crowds singing this 'alternative national anthem', as it's been called, are recognizing both that change comes when real longing is kindled and that the change we long for is already somehow inscribed in the very nature of things. Blake was enough of a true Christian prophet to cast this in terms of Jesus as a sign of God's faithful but so often hidden presence; and like any real poet he tries to find words for that moment when something shines forth through the clouds – the hope whose 'substance' as the Letter to the Hebrews puts it, is faith, trust in the God who has promised to be with us and among us – Satanic mills or no Satanic mills.

3 September

Law and order

'Each of us knows that our well-being is bound up with the well-being of our neighbours. And so every individual decision we make has to be made in full awareness of the implications for the whole community.'

A few years ago, I was taking part in a conference on prison policy in the UK. One of the speakers was an academic from New York who had spent a lot of time offering classes in law and philosophy in a local jail; and he said that one of the really eye-opening moments for him came when an inmate said, almost incredulously, 'You mean that the law is on *my side*?'

This man had only ever experienced law as law *enforcement*, as something that other people used to control and punish him. The idea that the law existed to protect him, and to guarantee that he had the same kind of security as everyone else, was revolutionary. The lecturer summed up his aims in prison education as trying to move people away from thinking about 'enforcement' and towards understanding the 'rule of law': the idea of a society in which the same protections are there for all, and no one disrupts that with impunity.

I thought of this earlier this week when speaking with a

(fellow) environmental protester in London. There's been a great deal of fuss about environmental activists breaking the law; but what struck me in this conversation – with someone who was very deliberately risking arrest – was that his main concern seemed to be *for* the rule of law in the fullest sense. When decisions were being made that rode roughshod over environmental needs, and very often over local protests as well, he said, there was a real problem about the rule of law: certain people were being granted immunity from real public scrutiny; choices were being made behind locked doors, dictated by short-term profit, which would have long-term human and ecological consequences. For him, law was about accountability, being open to public debate and questioning, so as to avoid the danger of greedy and corrupt groups or individuals endangering the common well-being of a society.

Opinions differ about the tactics of Extinction Rebellion and similar networks; I realize that not everybody thinks that a few middle-class activists getting arrested will change the world. But it matters quite a lot to see how the motivation of so many is the very opposite of individualistic anarchy, lawlessness. The American President may roll up the entire phenomenon of street protest in recent months under the heading of 'anarchy'; but – granted that sometime protests slip over into self-destructive violence and chaos – the real agenda of many protesters is that *the law should be honoured*.

Law enforcement officers have to be accountable for what they do; they should not be just one tribe in a tribal war. But travelling militias and agitators, vigilantes and provocateurs, whatever banner they march under, jeopardize any hope of genuine lawfulness. 'Defund the police' may not be the most helpful battle-cry, but if we agree with my New York colleague, we have to think of policing as *part* of a much wider programme of investing public resources that can help people (especially those who historically have no great reason to trust law enforcement representatives) to have confidence that the legal processes of society will be there to support and defend them.

And that means better, more intelligent investment in youth services and education and family support, not just more tools for forcibly controlling emergencies. As with so many social crises, the real question is how we make emergencies less likely. It's not a million miles away from the arguments in defence of public health regulations that we have got used to in recent months. Patient, small-scale policies of care and habits of attentiveness are essential to avoiding disasters that damage everyone.

There is a bad habit among Christians of repeating clichés about law and gospel, casting 'the law' as the villain (with a long-standing antisemitic undercurrent in this), standing over against the liberating and merciful gospel. But this is to misread Our Lord and St Paul: the idea that we can persuade God to be nice to us by keeping rules is every bit as silly as the Bible says – in the Old and New Testament alike. But the community created by God in the covenant made with Israel and in the invitation declared in the resurrection of Jesus and the gift of the Spirit is most emphatically a community of 'lawfulness' in the sense that each of us knows that our well-being is bound up with the well-being of our neighbours. And so every individual decision we make has to be made in full awareness of the implications for the whole community.

The Church, no less than the Israelites receiving the Torah from Moses, is a society in which mutual accountability is built into the very foundations of common life. This is a community part of whose purpose is to assure everyone that their interests are safe with their neighbour – that shared security is everyone's business and that no amount of wealth or status buys you impunity. Perhaps, as acrimonious debates about 'law and order' unfold in the UK and the USA, one of the contributions the Church should be making is to talk more about law as the condition for an honest and open society, a society of people who are determined that their neighbours should be secure and that no one's need goes unnoticed – a society where the law is truly on everyone's side.

10 September

The presence of the past

'Remembering our past involves something like letting light into more and more of the corners and byways of our identity; what returns in memory is now set in a larger landscape. We have learned; we have grown. The past is never over, but it is not everything.'

Life in our house at the moment is dominated by our forthcoming move to Wales. Every day brings new challenges in terms of getting rid of stuff – bits of furniture, photo albums, and, above all, books. It's been a particularly tough exercise deciding that some books I've treasured since my childhood will have to go. The new house is a good deal smaller, and it will help if we have some wall space not covered with bookshelves, so the pressure is on. Sometimes it feels like pressure to let go of precious bits of oneself, the distant self that loved reading this story or looking at this picture.

As it happens, I'm also currently involved in planning a conference next year on the art that's produced by migrants – a conference which, among other things, is looking at the sorts of objects migrants take with them when they travel, especially when they have to leave their homes with little or no notice because of war or other upheavals. My own experience gives a very small and almost trivial glimpse into the nature of losing things we treasure. For someone crossing land and sea to escape appalling trauma, these are losses that bite deep. And it is all the more important to recognize what sort of thoughts and feelings are going on when people decide that they *have* to take this or that with them: a toy, a piece of embroidered cloth, a well-worn household object, a picture of the view from the window.

It's not just about objects: people take with them their own language and stories, their music and their local crafts. It's all a powerful witness to the fact that our identity is never something independent of *where* we belong, *who* we belong with, *what* has made us human, *what* has made us this or that specific human. We don't own a polished and finished individual identity. We exist as a meeting point for all kinds of acts and processes and impressions, and all of those are what lives in us now. In the words of the great American writer, William Faulkner: 'The past isn't dead. It isn't even past.'

So the 'I' that is currently walking around, working, writing, talking, even sleeping is always a cluster of memories and experiences – not a neatly defined individual moving at a steady pace through life in a straight line. We've all had the experience of something activating a buried memory – and so a buried sense of who I am or who I was. It happens with terribly painful memories we'd rather not have – very much so with memories of abuse and violent damage. It happens also with joys and hopes. My past self or selves will live on, known or unknown. I might have thought I'd sorted out some aspect of my life, and then I find myself reacting to a challenge as my fourteen-year- old or thirty-year-old self – or indeed my two-year-old or six-month-old self. Not over, not even past.

That's of course why as a community of faith we don't let go of the past. We listen again to the narrative of the Bible – which itself is full of stories in which things that were supposed to be over and done with spring to life again in new situations. A prophet like Hosea can tell his contemporaries that they are still at some level living in the period of the rebellious, directionless wanderings in the desert after the Exodus, and they need to *recognize* the ways in which they're still stuck there so that God can speak to them again as he did to the people in the desert the first time round. The Gospels are full of this, as Jesus provokes responses that come from different eras and different contexts in Israel's past – responses of both love and panic in the face of the immediacy of God's compassion. And in the Eucharist, we deliberately bring to life the double memory of Jesus' friends betraying him and Jesus himself offering them hospitality, offering the bread from heaven that is his own life. *This* past is emphatically not past.

But the important thing here is that when the past is allowed to come to life in this dramatic way – in Hosea's preaching, in Jesus' suffering and dying – it's not to cancel out what has happened in the meantime. It's not what T. S. Eliot called 'ringing the bell backwards' and returning to where we were. Remembering our past involves something like letting light into more and more of the corners and byways of our identity; what returns in memory is now set in a larger landscape. We have learned; we have grown. The past is never over, but it is not everything.

A fierce clinging to what we have inherited from the past is never enough. We have to look at the new landscape and see freshly in this new setting what we remember. In the Church's life, it's the tightrope we tread between the amnesia that is so consumed by contemporary pressure and fashion that it never bothers to find out what the community's memory or tradition is saying, and the equally damaging traditionalism which idealizes the entity we think we once were. Both of these refuse the really creative challenge of integrating 'past selves' in a fuller understanding of the present.

'Christ yesterday and today', says the prayer over the Easter Candle which we were thinking about a few months ago; 'all times belong to him and all the ages.' He is contemporary with me now; and when I remember with honesty and hope, I discover that he is contemporary with what I remember, faithfully at work in my past as in my present. And as I struggle and pray to bring together the fragments of an identity that is always being shaken around and remodelled, I get some glimpse of the promised end in which Christ simply embraces the whole of me, all I have been, and makes it one with itself and with him.

17 September

Herd mentality

'If it's sinful and stupid to give way to mere conformity, it's equally sinful and stupid to think that the bare assertion of my individual will is the answer... . Healing and holiness come when we are gifted by Christ's Spirit to pick up the quiet hints, the shifts of movement and possibility, that will allow us to travel on together.'

In another of his creative adventures in the English language, President Trump a few days ago expressed his confidence that the COVID-19 pandemic would be dealt with by 'herd mentality'. It wasn't too difficult to work out what (I hope) he meant; and in fairness even the most experienced public figure might have some problems explaining exactly what 'herd immunity' in fact involves.

'Herd mentality' is, of course, a metaphor whose associations are entirely negative. We deplore people who (like lemmings – another standard image, now known to be libellously unfair to the poor creatures) never think for themselves, but follow the crowd; we admire those who stand out against the 'herd' and find their own path, decide on their own convictions. The herd is lazy and dim-witted, and the individual needs to resist. It's ironic that we still say we admire such people even in a society where mass conformity, mass surveillance and the mass market are the background of most human lives, where advertising algorithms work on the assumption that the only question that matters is really which herd we want to run with, and where social media increasingly works to create non-communicating tribes, or 'twitter mobs'.

The idea that humans face a choice between being bold individuals or stupid members of collectives is deeply engrained, and any religious believer might well want to ask a few awkward questions. Those questions were suddenly focused for me the other afternoon when, talking to a friend in the garden here, I saw a small group of geese flying overhead in beautiful and apparently effortless geometrical formation.

Flocks of migrating birds so often amaze by the complex mobile patterns they make, wheeling and spiralling in wonderful interweaving patterns like a cloth shifting and rippling in the wind, or a stream over stones. And I thought, 'Is this "herd mentality"? If so, perhaps we might just think again about the term.' Groups of animals and birds don't by any means always look as if they're stupidly following mindless social rules. Their collective life seems to reflect a kind of intelligence that is being deeply shared. And with some migrating birds, like geese, that intelligence imperceptibly shifts different birds to the front at different times, so that not all have to fly at the same pace all the time. Whatever is going on, it isn't some sort of mindless conformity.

It makes absolute sense to resist the notion that we should sacrifice our liberty and our reason to any kind of enforced collective mindset – and we ought to be a great deal more rebellious than we usually are about advertising, surveillance, fashion, echo chambers and all the ways in which this can happen. All of that feels like surrendering our precious uniqueness to something inferior, something less than human.

But what if the alternative were not just bloody-minded independence? (That wouldn't get you very far in a flock of migrating geese, any more than in a rugby team or a choir.) What if something like a human version of the migrating flock were possible? Somehow, each bird in the flock is alert to the movement of the others, subtly adjusting its flight to theirs; somehow, this intelligent awareness of the group produces harmony and beauty, and a sharing out of the burdens of significant work.

The Iona Community in Scotland famously speaks about itself in terms of the effort to realize something like the pattern of birds in flight together; their publishing house is called 'Wild Goose Publications', and the founder of the community, George MacLeod, often returned to the theme of how the flight of the geese was a sign of how shared leadership worked – now one, now another moving into the key position. In the Church, he said, instead of a single monolithic hierarchy and a single normative style of worship, we should be looking for a graceful readiness to let another take the lead and set the pace for a season. Movement together was not an army in lockstep but a flock wheeling and re-forming and moving on in glad responsiveness to one another – in shared and sanctified *intelligence.*

This is community life not as enforced conformity but as an *attentiveness*, so careful and sensitive that people learn how to flow around one another as they move, not surrendering to something subhuman but rising to a different level of human understanding and action. This surely is some of what we mean by the transfiguration of the individual into the *person*, with love and intelligence enhanced by the common life; the gift of the Spirit in the Body of Christ, a community where we become more human, more *ourselves*, in this deep shared understanding and responsiveness. If it's sinful and stupid to give way to mere conformity, it's equally sinful and stupid to think that the bare assertion of my individual will is the answer. 'I did it my way' may be popular on Desert Island Discs or at funerals, but it has its limits as a philosophy of life. Healing and holiness come when we are gifted by Christ's Spirit to pick up the quiet hints, the shifts of movement and possibility, that will allow us to travel on together.

Perhaps Donald Trump was right (not a sentence I am likely to write very often), and our ills really are cured by 'herd mentality' – by shared, interweaving intelligent, reciprocal action and movement. But in any case, take the opportunity this autumn to look at the birds flying south, and ask, 'What if human communities – what if *Christian* communities – could learn that kind of free thinking together and acting together?'

Epilogue

'The summer is ended and we are not saved' (Jeremiah 8.20). Anyone who remembers those bleak words from the prophet will probably feel that they have a harsh appropriateness just at present. We still don't know for how long we will have to live with this pandemic, what the eventual cost will be in lives, jobs, confidence, physical safety, mental and spiritual well-being. For all of us, some much more than others, the effects of the pandemic continue to bite deep.

Over-excited commentators are happy to hand out blame. Easy enough to do, and there are indeed some hard questions to be answered about slow and half-hearted responses and inflated claims. But it's a lot more difficult to acknowledge that we have genuinely been overtaken not only by practical challenges that no one had fully foreseen but by *feelings* no one had foreseen. Some of the more insightful commentators have noted that the pandemic has set a large question mark against the assumption of guaranteed security that has been the backdrop to the lives of more prosperous communities and individuals for decades – the narrative that we are steadily 'taming' our environment.

Most of the human race has not, of course, enjoyed that luxury anyway; and one thing that should come into focus in the light of the pandemic is this new and unwelcome solidarity in uncertainty. The British theologian Andrew

Shanks has written a good deal about 'the solidarity of the shaken' – the possibility of discovering real community on the far side of recognizing a vulnerability in which we're all involved.

That's one of the things that a community of faith might well be thinking about at the moment. The Christian gospel repeatedly tells us that we are always involved in a situation of shared failure and shared insecurity; it tells us that this is overcome only when we stop denying it by closing our hearts to each other; and it announces that our closed hearts can be and are broken open to each other through the action of God in Jesus and the Spirit. Faith does not deny the fragility we all share, nor does it make light of the cost and pain of it. It invites us to confront our shared fragility with honesty and compassion, recognizing our need of one another, our need for the neighbour to be well and safe – instead of falling back on our fearful attempts to be safe at the neighbour's expense.

Trust that we can face the truth without being destroyed; hope that the crisis we seem caught in is not the last word about what's possible for human beings; and love, the full-hearted will for the well-being of the entire world we inhabit. This is the landscape we live in, the landscape whose contours we have to try to make more real to those around us. The great question, as and when we have emerged from the immediate shadow of the pandemic, will be: What have we learned? Christians should be able to prompt, and to build on, some answers.

Perhaps we have learned more about our dependence on one another; perhaps we have learned something of the need to accept the limits and risks of living in a world we are never likely to tame successfully and totally. Or perhaps we have had our eyes opened to who is least safe in our neighbourhood – and not just our immediate neighbourhood, but our global neighbourhood: those who have never shared the security we take for granted; those who have lived for years with the isolation and frustration that we so chafe at; those whose jobs are the first to be lost; those enduring depression and other mental challenges; those with partners or relatives who've become mentally or physically abusive; those in front-line care work who have given their lives in the fight to control the virus; those who have lost loved ones either to the virus itself or because the treatment needed for other conditions could not be delivered in time.

Ultimately the question for us as a society is whether we have *grown* through the solidarity into which we have been forced. Simple solutions are not yet in sight as we move into a hard winter. But, to go back to the very first of these reflections, what if the change has already begun? What if something of a new world has been seen afresh and has kindled a new force of longing for generous, equitable, joyful living together?

Pray that it is so; act as if it were.

An easy way to get
to know the Bible

'For those who've been putting aside two years in later life
to read the Bible from cover to cover, the good news is: the
most important bits are here.' Jeremy Vine, BBC Radio 2

The Bible is full of dramatic stories that have made it the world's
bestselling book. But whoever has time to read it all from cover to
cover? Now here's a way of getting to know the Bible without having
to read every chapter and verse.

No summary, no paraphrase, no commentary: just the Bible's own
story in the Bible's own words.

'What an amazing concept! This
compelling, concise, slimmed-down
Scripture is a must for anyone who finds
those sixty-six books a tad daunting.'
Paul Kerensa, comedian
and script writer

'A great introduction to the main stories
in the Bible and it helps you to see how
they fit together. It would be great to give
as a gift.'
Five-star review on Amazon

The One Hour Bible
978 0 281 07964 3 • £4.99

 spck.org.uk /SPCKPublishing  @SPCKPublishing @SPCK_Publishing

WE HAVE A VISION OF A WORLD IN WHICH EVERYONE IS TRANSFORMED BY CHRISTIAN KNOWLEDGE

As well as being an award-winning publisher, SPCK is the oldest Anglican mission agency in the world.

Our mission is to lead the way in creating books and resources that help everyone to make sense of faith.

Will you partner with us to put good books into the hands of prisoners, great assemblies in front of schoolchildren and reach out to people who have not yet been touched by the Christian faith?

To donate, please visit www.spckpublishing.co.uk/donate or call our friendly fundraising team on 020 7592 3900.